GUNPLAY

By Robby McMurtry

The TRUE STORY of PISTOL PETE

on the HOOTOWL TRAIL

NEW FORUMS

Stillwater, Oklahoma
U.S.A.

NEW FORUMS PRESS INC.

Published in the United States of America
by New Forums Press, Inc.
1018 S. Lewis St.
Stillwater, OK 74074
www.newforums.com

Library of Congress Cataloging-in-Publication Data Pending

This book may be ordered in bulk quantities at discount from New Forums Press, Inc., P.O. Box 876, Stillwater, OK 74076 [Federal I.D. No. 73 1123239]. Printed in the United States of America.

International Standard Book Number: 1-58107-130-2

Cover design by Robby McMurtry.

Table of Contents

THIS IS FOR
BEN HARJO, JR.
ALIAS "SHORTY"

Special Thanks to
Diron Ahlquist of "Oklahombres"

IT CAN BE IMAGINED ON A MAP, THOUGH NONE WILL SHOW IT, WINDING OUT OF **OLD MEXICO**, ACROSS DESERTS AND RIVERS AND PLAINS, PARALLELLING **THE SANTA FE, CHISHOLM,** AND **KLONDIKE TRAILS,** THE NATCHEZ TRACE, EL CAMINO REAL. IT HAS A THOUSAND SIDETRACKS AND UNCOUNTED FOOTPATHS. MEN WHO TRAVEL IT DO SO BECAUSE THEY ARE "ON THE SCOUT," "ON THE DODGE," AT RIGHT ANGLES TO THE **LAW,** AND IT LEADS TO EVERY BOOMTOWN, LINE SHACK, RESERVATION AND ROBBERS' ROOST. ITS TRAVELERS HAVE NAMES THAT ARE NOT THEIR OWN AND SEE STRANGE SHADOWS THAT COULD BE THEMSELVES. THEY SMELL OF **WOODSMOKE** AND **PONIES** AND **WILDERNESS** WHEN TRAVELING

The Hootowl Trail.

MEN WHO TRAVEL IT FEAR **BLIND MEN** AFOOT...
... MEDITATE AND PRAY OVER A SINGLE **FOOTPRINT...**
... WATCH THE **MOON** SWELL AND GROW THIN...
... KNOW THE MILKY WAY, THE PLEIADES, MORNING STAR...
... EAT AT THE HOMES OF THE REMOTE **POOR** AND BECOME STILL IN THE HOUR WHEN SHADOWS GROW LONG.

THEY SLEEP IN RUNNING **DREAMS** AND WAKE IN NAMELESS HILLS, KNOWING — EVEN AS THEY SELL PIECES OF THEMSELVES —

SOMEONE IS BEHIND THEM.

①

Osage County,

KANSAS
1868

THE WAR BETWEEN THE STATES
HAS BRED A GENERATION OF MEN, ARMED AND HUNGRY,
WHO SWARM OUT ONTO THE PLAINS.

MOSE BEAMAN

MOSES (MOSE) BEAMAN WAS BORN IN 1812 IN
CONNECTICUT. IN 1849, HE WENT TO CALIF-
ORNIA AS A PARTICIPANT IN THE GOLD RUSH.
  HE SETTLED WITH HIS WIFE AND FAMILY
IN KANSAS, NEAR THE SANTA FE TRAIL,
IN 1857.
  FRANK EATON, PISTOL PETE, SAID BEAMAN
WAS "THE MAN WHO LEARNED ME HOW TO
SHOOT."

Samuel Colt's Revolver

"GOD CREATED MAN, BUT SAM COLT MADE THEM EQUAL."
—AMERICAN PROVERB

GUN MANUFACTURERS HAD ATTEMPTED TO DESIGN MULTIPLE-SHOT HANDGUNS BEFORE SAMUEL COLT PRODUCED HIS FIVE-SHOT REVOLVER IN 1835. THE GUN WAS PROVEN IN BATTLE WHEN USED BY TEXAS RANGERS AGAINST THE COMANCHES IN THE 1840's, ALTHOUGH IT DID NOT BECOME WELL-KNOWN AT THAT TIME.

IN 1848, THE UNITED STATES GOVERNMENT PURCHASED ONE THOUSAND OF COLT'S SIX-SHOT REVOLVERS FOR USE IN THE MEXICAN WAR, AND BY 1855 HIS PATENT ARMS MANUFACTURING CO. WAS THE LARGEST PRIVATE GUN MANUFACTURER IN THE WORLD. DURING THE WAR BETWEEN THE STATES, THE REVOLVER BECAME WIDELY POPULAR.

THE FIRST REVOLVERS FIRED ROUND BALLS, WHICH WERE RAMMED HOME AFTER A POWDER CHARGE HAD BEEN PLACED IN EACH CYLINDER. IN THE LATE 1860's, GUNSMITHS BEGAN CONVERTING THE CAP-AND-BALL SIXSHOOTERS TO FIRE THE NEW CARTRIDGE AMMUNITION, WHICH MEANT THE SHOOTER COULD RELOAD MUCH FASTER. THESE CONVERSIONS, ESPECIALLY THE ARMY AND NAVY MODELS, WERE SERIOUS FIGHTING HANDGUNS THROUGHOUT THE WEST.

IN 1873, THE COLT PEACEMAKER, MANUFACTURED SOLELY FOR USE WITH CARTRIDGES, CAME INTO USE. SMITH & WESSON AND REMINGTON REVOLVERS WERE ALSO WIDESPREAD ON THE FRONTIER, BUT COLT'S FIREARMS WERE, AND REMAIN, FAVORITES.

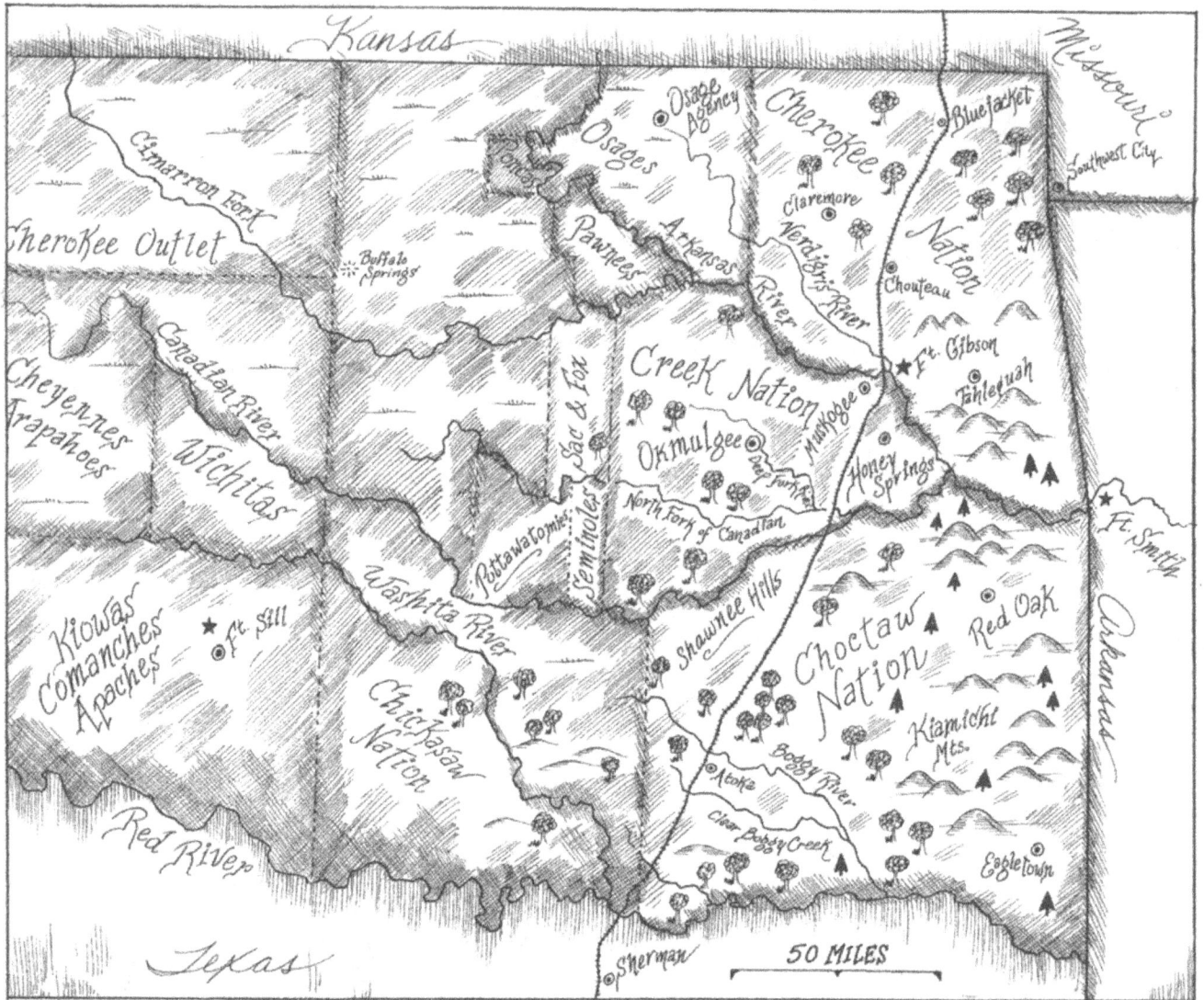

Indian Territory 1877

ON THE EDGE OF AMERICA —
THE FINAL HOME OF THE TRIBES
AND A REFUGE FOR DESPERADOES —

Fort Gibson,
Cherokee Nation

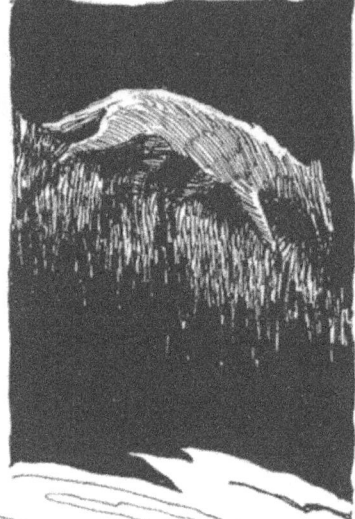

Osage Reservation

PETE, THIS MAN FOREMAN, BIG **BOSS**, NAME George Goodin!

PLEASED TO MEET YOU, **PETE!** NOT A BAD-LOOKIN' BUNCH OF NAGS, **JIM!** I'LL GIVE YOU **SIX** DOLLARS A HEAD!

MAKE IT **EIGHT** DOLLARS, MR. GOODIN, AND WE'LL **BREAK** 'EM FOR YOU!

ALRIGHT, BOYS, PUT 'EM IN THE PEN AND GO TO **WORK!**

TOSS YOUR GEAR IN THE BUNKHOUSE!

DUST—

HOT BREATH AND SWEAT—

A SQUEAL OF FEAR—

FULL OF FIRE—

WILDER THAN LIGHTNING—

AND AN ANGEL WATCHES—

RIDE OUT THE STORM—

RIDE THROUGH THE NIGHT—

RIDE DOWN THE MOON—

THEY CAN LIVE— ONLY AS LONG AS THEY CAN HIDE—

Winchester Repeating Arms Co.

"Load on Sunday and shoot all week!"

CHRISTOPHER SPENCER'S LEVER-ACTION REPEATING RIFLES AND CARBINES WERE PROVEN IN COMBAT BY THE UNION ARMY CAVALRY DURING THE WAR BETWEEN THE STATES.

AFTER THE WAR, OLIVER WINCHESTER GAINED CONTROL OF THE MANUFACTURING FACILITIES AND ESTABLISHED THE WINCHESTER REPEATING ARMS COMPANY.

IN 1866, THE FIRST WINCHESTER RIFLE, AN IMPROVED DESIGN BASED ON THE SPENCER MODEL, WAS PRODUCED.

LATER MODELS USED THE .44-40 CALIBER AMMUNITION, WHICH WAS INTERCHANGEABLE WITH THE POPULAR COLT REVOLVERS, AND THE REMINGTON REPEATER WAS CONSTANTLY REFINED AND IMPROVED.

EVERYONE WHO CARRIED A WINCHESTER — PEACE OFFICERS, HUNTERS, DESPERADOES, FARMERS, CATTLEMEN, SHEEP MEN, INDIANS — FOUND IT TO BE A DEPENDABLE AND INDISPENSEABLE WEAPON. AS A PRACTICAL MATTER, THE LONGARM WAS MORE USEFUL AND MORE ACCURATE — ESPECIALLY FROM A DISTANCE — THAN ANY HANDGUN.

REMINGTON RIFLES WERE WIDELY USED IN LATER EUROPEAN CONFLICTS, AND THE GUN HAS ENTERED WORLDWIDE MYTHOLOGY AS THE QUINTESSENTIAL WEAPON OF THE AMERICAN FRONTIER.

MANY OF THE ORIGINAL RIFLE MODELS ARE STILL IN PRODUCTION.

Lighthorse

AROUND THE TIME OF THE WAR BETWEEN THE STATES, THE CHEROKEE, CHOCTAW, SEMINOLE, CREEK, AND CHICKASAW NATIONS FORMED MOUNTED POLICE UNITS KNOWN AS LIGHTHORSE.

THE LIGHTHORSE PURSUED STOCK THIEVES, ROBBERS, AND MURDERERS AND ENFORCED TRIBAL LAW. THEY FREQUENTLY INTERCEPTED WHISKY PEDDLERS, FORCING THEM TO POUR THE ILLEGAL LIQUOR ON THE GROUND.

LAWBREAKERS COULD BE WHIPPED, HAVE THEIR EARS CUT OFF AND, OCCASIONALLY, BE EXECUTED WITH A BULLET TO THE HEART.

Sam Sixkiller

A VETERAN OF THE CIVIL WAR, SAM SIXKILLER WAS FROM THE GOINGSNAKE DISTRICT OF THE CHEROKEE NATION. IN 1880, HE BECAME THE FIRST CAPTAIN OF THE UNITED STATES INDIAN POLICE, COORDINATING THE ACTIVITIES OF THE LIGHTHORSE POLICEMEN. HE WAS ALSO CROSS-DEPUTIZED AS A U.S. DEPUTY MARSHAL, AND HE WORKED AS A SPECIAL AGENT FOR THE MISSOURIPACIFIC RAILROAD.

SIXKILLER KILLED THE INFAMOUS OUTLAW, DICK GLASS, AND APPREHENDED MANY NOTORIOUS HORSETHIEVES AND BOOTLEGGERS.

SIXKILLER WAS UNARMED WHEN, ON CHRISTMAS EVE 1886, HE WAS GUNNED DOWN IN MUSKOGEE.

Southwest City, Missouri

"Hell on the Border"

Judge Parker's Federal Court at Fort Smith, Arkansas

IN 1875, ISAAC PARKER WAS APPOINTED FEDERAL JUDGE FOR THE WESTERN DISTRICT OF ARKANSAS, WITH JURISDICTION OVER NEARLY 80,000 SQUARE MILES OF INDIAN TERRITORY; THE AREA WAS INFESTED WITH RENEGADES— WHITE, BLACK, AND RED.

IN HIS FIRST YEAR AT FORT SMITH, PARKER HANGED ELEVEN MEN, EARNING HIMSELF THE NICKNAME "THE HANGING JUDGE."

OVER THE TWENTY-ONE YEARS HE PRESIDED, NO FEWER THAN SIXTY-FIVE OF HIS DEPUTY MARSHALS WERE KILLED IN THE LINE OF DUTY, AND PARKER SENTENCED 172 OUTLAWS TO DEATH.

WHEN PARKER PASSED AWAY IN 1896, THE FORT SMITH JAIL HELD MORE THAN FIFTY CONVICTED MURDERERS.

HILLS OLD AS CREATION —
WHERE DISTANCES ARE LOST —

WHERE ANY MAN COULD BE
A VICIOUS DOG —

NO ONE IS BORN WITH A DUTY TO ANYONE ELSE—

AND HOW LONG A MAN LIVES HAS NOTHING TO DO WITH HOW LONG HE'S DEAD—

GOOD AFTERNOON! CAN YOU TELL ME WHERE I MIGHT FIND JONCE CAMPSEY?

MY NAME'S SMITH!

I DON'T KNOW ANYBODY NAMED CAMPSEY!

I HAVE A MESSAGE FROM DOC FERBER, AND I'M NOT TO GIVE IT TO ANYONE... EXCEPT JONCE CAMPSEY!

I'M JONCE CAMPSEY!..

...THIS IS MY BROTHER, JIM! WHAT DID DOC SAY?

I'M FRANK EATON, AND DOC SAID HE'D SEE YOU IN HELL!

Cattle Ranching in the Indian Nations

BY THE LATE 1870's, WHEN FREE GRAZING LAND HAD BECOME SCARCE ELSEWHERE, RANCHING ASSOCIATIONS BEGAN LEASING VAST TRACTS OF GRASSLAND FROM THE INDIAN NATIONS. SOME CATTLEMEN TOOK INDIAN WIVES AND ESTABLISHED LARGE RANCHES, EMPLOYING INDIAN FOREMEN AND COWBOYS.

SEVERAL CATTLE RANCHES OPERATED ON THE OPEN RANGES OF THE SIX-MILLION-ACRE CHEROKEE OUTLET, NEAR THE KANSAS BORDER. MOST OPERATIONS WERE REMOTE, FAR FROM TOWNS OR LAW, AND PRIVATE RANGE DETECTIVES WERE EMPLOYED TO DEAL WITH THE CONSTANT PROBLEM OF LIVESTOCK THEFT. THIEVES WERE OFTEN REMANDED TO THE CUSTODY OF FEDERAL MARSHALS, BUT SOMETIMES JUSTICE WAS SUMMARILY DEALT BY BULLET OR NOOSE.

IN THE 1880's AND '90's, RANCHERS IN THE INDIAN NATIONS WERE ALLIES OF THE TRIBAL GOVERNMENTS IN OPPOSING OPENING THE TERRITORY TO WHITE HOMESTEADERS.

SOMEWHERE —

A COYOTE IS SINGING —

AND A NIGHTBIRD ASKS —

WHO IS THERE?

OH..!

I'M SORRY... I DIDN'T MEAN TO SPOOK YOU!

STAY WITH HER, PETE!

RIDE HER DOWN, BOY!

#!!@#...

?

HO! WHAT'S WRONG, BOSS?

#@! IF IT'S NOT CATTLE THIEVES, IT'S DAMN HORSE THIEVES...

...SOMEBODY'S APPROPRIATING OUR COW PONIES UP ON BIRD CREEK! I WANT YOU BOYS TO RIDE THE LINE AND FIND OUT WHO!

IF MEN AND HORSES WERE GHOSTS—

THEY MIGHT PASS OVER THE EARTH WITHOUT LEAVING A MARK—

BUT MEN RIDE AND HORSES RUN—

AND THERE ARE ALWAYS—

SIGNS OF THEIR PASSING.

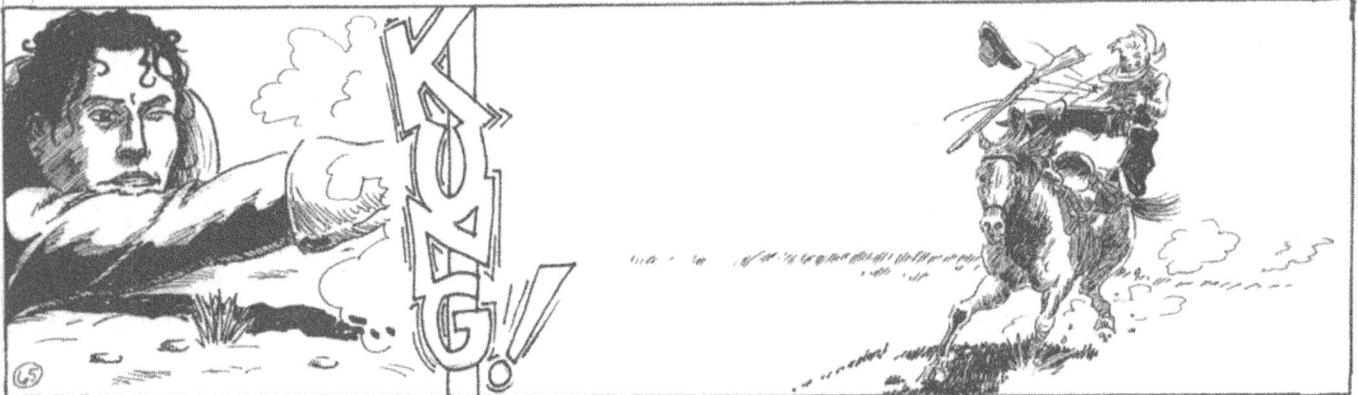

HAA, WAS-TE LA!

HE SAYS THAT **WAKAN** – THE **CREATOR** – SET US ON THE WORLD A LONG, LONG TIME AGO!... AND HE TOLD THE **PEOPLE**: "YOU WILL LIVE MANY YEARS, MAYBE, BUT ALL THINGS – ALL **PEOPLE** – MUST **DIE** SOME TIME. WHEN THAT HAPPENS – WHEN YOU **DIE**, I WILL SET YOU IN THE SKY AS A **STAR**, AND YOU CAN LOOK DOWN AND SEE YOUR **LOVED ONES** WHO STILL **LIVE!**"... HE SAYS THAT WHEN YOU ARE OUT IN THE **NIGHT**, AND THE SKY IS **CLEAR**, LOOK **UP**, AT THE ONES WHO WENT BEFORE YOU – THE **GRANDMOTHERS**, THE BROTHERS, SISTERS AND **LOVED** ONES WHO ARE WATCHING YOU...

The Osage

Children of the Middle Waters

THE OSAGE, WHO CALL THEMSELVES WA-SHA-ZHE, LIVED IN WHAT IS NOW MISSOURI WHEN FIRST DESCRIBED BY WHITE EXPLORERS. BY THE EARLY 1600's THEY WERE CLOSELY ALLIED, AND INTIMATE WITH, FRENCH TRADERS.

AS THE AMERICAN FRONTIER ADVANCED, THE OSAGE, DECIMATED BY WARFARE AND DISEASE, WERE PUSHED WESTWARD, WHERE THEY CAME INTO CONFLICT WITH THE CHEROKEES AND PLAINS TRIBES. MANY OSAGES WERE EMPLOYED AS GUIDES AND SCOUTS BY THE U. S. ARMY.

AFTER THE WAR BETWEEN THE STATES, THE OSAGE WERE REMOVED FROM KANSAS TO A TWO-MILLION-ACRE RESERVATION IN INDIAN TERRITORY. LATER, MANY TRIBAL MEMBERS BECAME FABULOUSLY WEALTHY WHEN OIL WAS DISCOVERED THERE.

OSAGE NATION TRIBAL HEADQUARTERS IS LOCATED IN PAWHUSKA. OKLAHOMA.

MELANCHOLY DAWN - MOCKINGBIRDS SING GOODBYE -

FRANK, I WANT YOU TO WEAR THIS... AND I WANT YOU TO BRING IT BACK TO ME!

I PROMISE...

MOST YOUNG MANS THINK THEY GOING TO LIVE **FOREVER!** PETE KNOWS HE MIGHT DIE **ANY** TIME!

EVERY MAN IS SEARCHING FOR SOMETHING - AND EVERY JOURNEY HAS ITS OWN REASONS -

Albuquerque, New Mexico Territory 1881

Fort Wingate
Santa Fe
Santo Domingo Pueblo
Rio Grande (River)
Cimarron Territory
Unorganized - No Man's Land
Albuquerque
Tucumcari
Los Pinos Mountains
Fort Sumner
Bosque Redondo
Socorro
Rio Grande (River)
Jornada del Muerto
Chupadera Mesa
Fort Stanton
Pecos River
Llano Estacado
Texas

ACROSS THE PRAIRIES, BEYOND THE PLAINS —

IN THIS LAND OF SUN, SAND, AND BLISTERS —

SURELY FINAL VENGEANCE IS HERE —

Pat Garrett

PAT GARRETT WAS A BUFFALO HUNTER, COWBOY, AND BARTENDER BEFORE HE WAS ELECTED SHERIFF OF LINCOLN COUNTY, NEW MEXICO IN 1880, AND IT WAS IN THAT CAPACITY THAT HE TRACKED DOWN AND KILLED WILLIAM BONNEY, BETTER KNOWN AS BILLY THE KID.

GARRETT WAS UNSUCCESSFUL AS A RANCHER, BUT HE WAS A CATTLE DETECTIVE AND RANGER IN TEXAS BEFORE BEING SLAIN BY AN UNKNOWN ASSASSIN IN 1908.

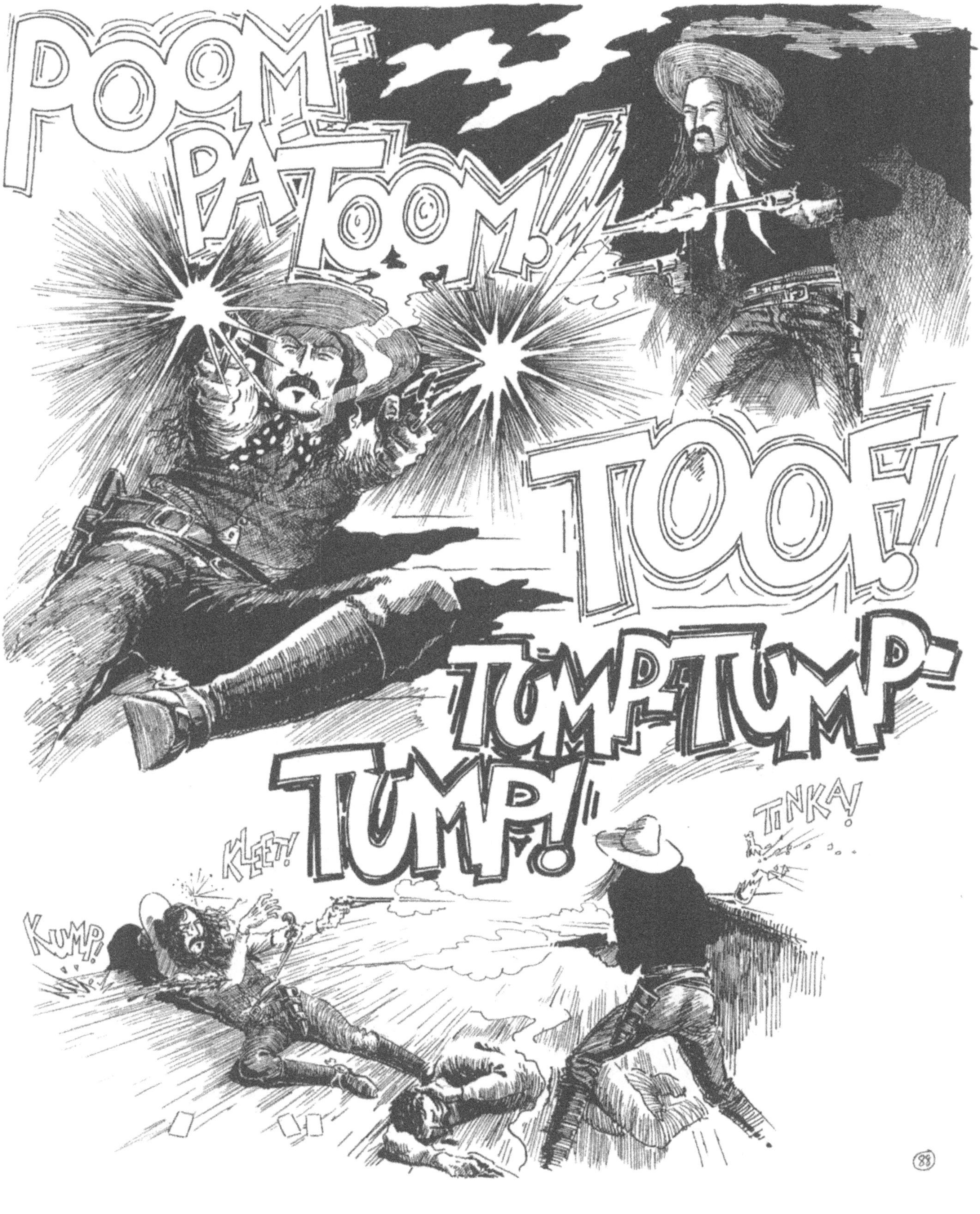
POOM-PATOOM!
TOOF!
TUMP-TUMP-
TUMP!
KLEET!
TINKA!
KUMP!

A MAN MAKES CAMP—
BUT A WOMAN

"AND NOW,
    LOOKING BACK OVER THE LONG TRAIL
                        OF LIFE...
HAS THE GAME BEEN WORTH
                    THE CANDLE?
I THINK I WOULD TAKE THE
                        HAND
AND PLAY IT
AGAIN."

        —FRANK "PISTOL PETE" EATON
                    APRIL 1958

It Could have Happened, So it Must be True

"IT IS NOT DEEDS OR ACTS THAT LAST, BUT THE WRITTEN RECORD OF THOSE DEEDS AND ACTS."

— ELBERT HUBBARD

OLD AGE, IT IS SAID, MAKES A MAN A STRANGER IN HIS OWN COUNTRY, AND FRANK "PISTOL PETE" EATON WAS A VERY OLD MAN WHEN HE DIED, CLAIMING TO BE 97 YEARS OLD, IN 1958. FOR MANY YEARS PRIOR TO HIS DEATH, AS THE FRONTIER AND ITS CAVALIERS RECEDED DEEPER INTO THE COLLECTIVE MEMORY OF AMERICA, EATON REMINISCED ABOUT THE WILD, OLD, WEST — COLORFUL, DANGEROUS, AND DIRTY — FILTERED THROUGH THE IMAGINATION OF THE DECADES.

AS AN OLD MAN, EATON SAW HIS IMAGE ADOPTED AS AN EMBLEM BY OKLAHOMA STATE UNIVERSITY IN STILLWATER, OKLAHOMA (LATER, IT WAS ADAPTED BY NEW MEXICO STATE UNIVERSITY AND THE UNIVERSITY OF WYOMING.); HE TOLD HIS TALES TO RAPT LISTENERS AND DICTATED HIS AUTOBIOGRAPHY; HE GAVE RADIO INTERVIEWS AND QUICK-DRAW DEMONSTRATIONS AT THE OKLAHOMA STATE UNIVERSITY STUDENT UNION, WHERE HE SHOT A HOLE IN THE WALL. HIS PISTOL, WHICH HAD ELEVEN NOTCHES, WAS STOLEN THERE.

EATON OPERATED A BLACKSMITH SHOP IN PERKINS, OKLAHOMA. HE WAS TWICE MARRIED AND HE FATHERED TEN CHILDREN. IN THE 1940'S HE RODE HORSEBACK FROM TEXAS TO KANSAS AS PART OF A WAR BOND CAMPAIGN.

EVEN THOUGH EATON'S STORIES CONTAIN SOME CIRCUMSTANTIAL EVIDENCE AND SEEM TO RING WITH AUTHENTIC DETAIL, MOST SERIOUS HISTORIANS DISMISS THEM AS REAL HISTORY, CITING AN ALMOST TOTAL LACK OF DOCUMENTATION OR CORROBORATION. ON THE OTHER HAND, MANY PEOPLE — INCLUDING ANGIE DEBO, WELL-KNOWN HISTORIAN — WHO MET EATON WERE ABSOLUTELY CONVINCED OF HIS AUTHENTICITY.

BOTH ARGUMENTS MAY BE IRRELEVANT. PISTOL PETE, CRACK SHOT OR CRACKPOT, HAS, IN REGIONAL MYTHOLOGY, BECOME AN ITEM IN THE PANTHEON OF AMERICAN GUNSLINGERS — AND HE OUTLIVED ALL THE OTHERS. HE WAS A RELIC.

EATON HIMSELF WROTE THAT HIS STORY WAS TRUE, BUT PEOPLE COULD "TAKE IT OR LEAVE IT ALONE, AS THEY PLEASE." OSCAR WILDE, EATON'S CONTEMPORARY, SAID THAT "HISTORY IS MERELY GOSSIP."

PISTOL PETE WAS AN OLD-TIMER WHO COULD TELL ABOUT HIS MANY INTERESTING ADVENTURES, AND SOME OF THEM MIGHT HAVE REALLY HAPPENED.

AN INFORMAL BIBLIOGRAPHY

BAKER, ELMER _GUNMAN'S TERRITORY_ NAYLOR CO., SAN ANTONIO TX: 1969

BURTON, ART _BLACK, RED, AND DEADLY_ EAKIN PRESS, AUSTIN TX: 1991

CRUTCHFIELD, O'NEAL, WALKER _LEGENDS OF THE WILD WEST_ PUBLICATIONS INTERNATIONAL, LINCOLNWOOD, IL: 1995

DALE, EDWARD EVERETT _COW COUNTRY_ OKLAHOMA UNIVERSITY PRESS, NORMAN OK: 1942

DAVIS, WILLIAM _THE AMERICAN FRONTIER_ SMITHMARK, NEW YORK, NY: 1992

EATON, FRANK _PISTOL PETE: VETERAN OF THE OLD WEST_ LITTLE, BROWN, AND CO., BOSTON MA: 1952

HOGG, IAN _THE COMPLETE ILLUSTRATED ENCYCLOPEDIA OF THE WORLD'S FIREARMS_, A & W PUBLISHERS, NEW YORK, NY: 1978

HOGG, IAN _THE COMPLETE HANDGUN 1300 TO THE PRESENT_ PHOEBUS PUBLISHING, LONDON ENGLAND: 1979

MATTHEWS, JOHN JOSEPH _THE OSAGES: CHILDREN OF THE MIDDLE WATERS_ UNIVERSITY OF OKLAHOMA PRESS, NORMAN OK: 1961

MAY, ROBIN _GUNFIGHTERS_ FREDERICK FELL PUBLISHERS, NEW YORK NY: 1983

SHIRLEY, GLENN _TOUGHEST OF THEM ALL_ UNIVERSITY OF NEW MEXICO PRESS: 1953

WALKER, PAUL _TRAIL OF THE WILD WEST_ NATIONAL GEOGRAPHIC SOCIETY, WASHINGTON D.C.: 1997

ARCHIVAL MATERIALS: FRANK EATON COLLECTION, OKLAHOMA STATE UNIVERSITY, STILLWATER, OK. LETTERS, INTERVIEWS, DOCUMENTS, NEWSPAPER AND MAGAZINE ARTICLES RE: FRANK EATON (PRIMARY SOURCES)

www.ingramcontent.com/pod-product-compliance
Lightning Source LLC
Chambersburg PA
CBHW080520090426
42734CB00015B/3116